Grace
IN THE EMPTY SPACES

Transformed by the One-Another Passages

MARK MCPEAK
WITH EMILY WHITE YOUREE

randall house

114 Bush Rd | Nashville, TN 37217
randallhouse.com

TABLE OF CONTENTS

INTRODUCTION

Church is meant to be one of those real-life places that both reveal and shape us. As with our families, the Lord intentionally puts us into a church as our spiritual family. He connects us with other people, and we experience life together. We live together with purpose—to reveal who God is by the way we interact with and love each other. Our interaction in the church is meant to be so powerful that it's magnetic.

Ouch!

The reputation and reality is that churches are often relational messes. Individuals may look at the way church members interact with each other and with outsiders and wonder why anyone would ever attend church. Like so many families, churches can become places of conflict, dysfunction, and pain. People disappoint and let each other down. They may be immature, inconsiderate, selfish, or just downright mean. How many have rejected Christ or never really considered the gospel message because of negative relationships in the Church?

But, this is not the way God intended it. He meant for church to be a wonderful, accepting, and encouraging place where hurts are healed and people become reflections of Jesus Christ. He still intends for His Church, the Body of Christ, to be such a place. This study is about God shaping you into the kind of person who can make His Church (your church) that wonderful place.

THE CHALLENGE OF CHRIST-LIKENESS

If churches are ever going to be wonderful, accepting, and nurturing places, they must be filled with people who reflect those qualities. And, that is precisely God's design. He wants to take our weaknesses and our tendencies to mess up relationships and totally transform us.

Paul, the apostle and church planter, emphasizes this transformation throughout his writings. Think about this concept as you read this selection of verses:

Romans 12:2	Do not be conformed to this world, but be transformed by the renewal of your mind.
2 Corinthians 5:17	Therefore, if anyone is in Christ, he is a new creation. The old has passed away; behold, the new has come.
Galatians 2:20	I have been crucified with Christ. It is no longer I who live, but Christ who lives in me. And the life I now live in the flesh I live by faith in the Son of God, who loved me and gave Himself for me.
Ephesians 4:22-24	To put off your old self, which belongs to your former manner of life and is corrupt through deceitful desires, and to be renewed in the spirit of your minds, and to put on the new self, created after the likeness of God in true righteousness and holiness.

Families and churches are places of hurt because people, by nature, tend to hurt each other. Without Christ in our lives, we are inclined to be selfish and hurtful. Being a follower of Christ should involve a dramatic change, a transformation—as Paul describes. In these verses, he is not talking about coming to know Jesus as your Savior. These verses are written to people who are already Christians. They are describing the process of change taking place in the life of a Christ-follower. If you have a relationship with

Jesus Christ and have been redeemed by what He did for you on the cross, His plan for you is to transform and make you like Him in every way.

JESUS—THE ULTIMATE PSYCHOLOGIST

No one understands human behavior and the human psyche like Jesus. He alone has the power to change us. He created us (Colossians 1:15–17) and knows everything about our needs. And, let's be honest, He also knows how we tend to hurt each other. There are often empty spaces between us—times when we don't know why someone said or did something. Our sinful nature is inclined to fill these spaces with suspicion, anger, or other negative assumptions. So much bitterness and hurt are the result. But, God has a different plan for these spaces. His grace transforms us and helps us fill these empty spaces between us with good. So, when Jesus gives instructions about human happiness, we would be wise to listen and follow His teachings.

In His first public message, Jesus provided deep insight into the motivations and practices that will make people blessed and happy (Matthew 5). These ideas, from what is commonly referred to as the Sermon on the Mount, represent the character qualities the transformation process is to produce in the Christ-follower. And, these are the basis for all of the one-another teachings we will be studying together.

When we refer to the "one-another passages" in this study, we are being literal. In many Bible translations, the verses we'll be studying are actually translated using the phrases "one-another." In some translations however, the text may read "each other" or use the word "others." When we think about how we, as followers of Christ, are to relate to each other, no passages are more instructive than these one-another verses.

❖ Loving people love others compassionately.

❖ Humble people submit to others meekly.

❖ Spiritual people pray for others passionately.

❖ Unselfish people serve other generously.

REAL CHANGE

Living out the one-another passages in the New Testament is much less about what we do than about who we are. It's possible to reduce these instructions to "rules of conduct" for the Christian. But, doing so misses the point. To look at these verses as rules is to make them transactional; we can count how many times we have "performed" a good deed for another.

Remember Jesus' many frustrations with the popular religious thinking of His day? He was particularly unhappy with the idea that goodness was simply about conduct. Jesus taught that real transformation is not about obeying the rules; it is much deeper and more real. He said, "The good person out of the good treasure of his heart produces good" (Luke 6:45a).

God's intention in the one-another passages is not about transactions or acts, but about transformation. He wants to make you and me into people who naturally live out the one-another passages as we interact with other believers. The one-another passages are about becoming and being the kind of person who naturally focuses on other people.

Do you want real change?

Do you want to be blessed?

Do you want your life to reflect Christ and be a blessing to others?

If so, this study is for you!

Mark McPeak

WEEK ONE
LOVE ONE ANOTHER

"A NEW COMMANDMENT I GIVE TO YOU, THAT YOU LOVE ONE ANOTHER: JUST AS I HAVE LOVED YOU, YOU ARE ALSO TO LOVE ONE ANOTHER" (JOHN 13:34).

For years, Jack's ultimate response to conflict was "that's just the way I am! If you don't like it, too bad." The pain of his past and Jack's responses to it always made him a difficult person to be around. A few times he talked about his past and attitudes, but it was always so painful, too painful. Life became easier if he avoided those talks.

When he was younger, Jack once prayed, "Jesus, I know You died on the cross for me. I am a sinner. I am sorry. Will You forgive me and make me Yours?" He has been in church since that prayer, even filling various roles and positions.

When he wakes up in the middle of the night and can't go back to sleep, Jack sometimes wonders if things really are "better," or if he has just grown so numb he doesn't care anymore. Does God love him? Does anyone love him? Does he love anyone? Jack doesn't know the answers, and isn't sure if really wants to know.

Does Jack's story sound like anyone you know? Have you ever felt like him? God does want to say something to and change something in Jack and those who struggle with similar thoughts and relational problems, especially those He calls His own.

God has grace for those empty spaces in our lives—those areas where we feel misunderstood and unloved personally and for those areas where we are neglecting and abusing our Christian family. In fact, in all of our relationships, God has provided a "recipe" for success, for glorifying Him, especially in our relationships with other brothers and sisters in Christ.

1. In the verses below, what is the overarching theme?

Mark 12:33

1 Thessalonians 4:9

2 John 1:5

The attribute of God that He most wants us to reflect and that He teaches us through His modeling is: *to love one another*. Love is the foundation of all the one-another passages. No one can genuinely serve, forgive, submit to, or pray for another unless love is present.

2. What does John 13:34-35; 15:12 teach regarding the type of love we are to exhibit?

It is easy for us to spend our lives comparing ourselves with others. In regard to loving, we test our love against that demonstrated by Jesus Christ.

3. According to John 3:16 and Romans 5:8, how has God loved us?

The primary commandment for the Christian, the outward symbol for everyone to see, is love. We should love each other in the same way He loved us.

It is easy to get lost in all the meanings of "love," especially in our English language. Yet, when we speak of God's love, which is the type of love we are to reflect, what does that love mean or look like exactly?

4. Read 1 Corinthians 13:1-13, and then write—in your own words—the definition of godly love:

❖ Seeing 1 Corinthians 13 embroidered on pillows or hearing it read at weddings may make this passage seem like a nice poem or cliché. However, it is a picture of the way God loves. He means it to be a description of the way His people love as well.

When reading the likes of Romans 5:8 and 1 Corinthians 13, it is tempting to become discouraged because we know how unloving we can be to our families, not even counting God's family! In light of that frustration and reality, it is important to remember that loving one another is not a works-oriented to-do list, but it is a heart issue. Remember, we are only redeemed because Christ makes us so. We are only holy because Christ makes us so. Thus, we can only be loving because Christ makes us so.

5. Relate a time when a fellow Christian has shown you godly love. What was the situation? How did you feel to receive such? What impact did it have in your life? How did you respond?

❖ Veteran missionary to India, Trula Cronk, related a story from her early Christian life to her college Sunday school class. She knew God wanted her to show love to someone who was, for her, completely unlovable. It was at that time God taught her one of the lessons about Christ-likeness. It was as though God was saying "just act like you love her, and I will do the rest." Her obedience to treat the person with love was accompanied by the grace of God that turned Trula's repulsion to love. "He wants to love through us when we cannot love on our own."

4

DAY 2: A PURE HEART

1. Write out 1 Peter 1:22.

2. What do you think is significant in this verse?

Peter reminds us of God's design for us—to be holy like He is. First Peter 1:15 says, "but as he who called you is holy, you also be holy in all your conduct." Just a few verses later (18–19), Peter then tells us the resource that can enable us to emulate His holiness—the power of the blood of Christ to make us righteous and holy, not just in our position before God, but in our daily living.

So, as we appropriate the power of the blood of Christ to help us live in purity and holiness, we are called (commanded) to love each other with an "earnest" love. The King James Version uses the word *fervently*, meaning to love with intensity. This is a love that seeks the good of another; it is intentional and active.

❖ "Knowing that you were ransomed from the futile ways inherited from your forefathers, not with perishable things such as silver or gold, but with the precious blood of Christ, like that of a lamb without blemish or spot" (1 Peter 1:18–19).

In verse 22, the phrase, "from a pure heart" literally means a "clean heart." God, through Christ has made us clean. We are to walk in purity/holiness and actively, passionately love each other with this clean heart God has given us. It takes a clean heart, cleansed by the power of Christ and kept clean through walking with Him daily to love as He loves. This is His will for the Church.

3. Write out 1 Peter 4:8.

Based on the "pure heart" from 1 Peter 1:22, the effect of our loving each other is a lessening of the impact and consequences of sin. The work of God in our hearts makes us like Him, meaning we do not try to expose or condemn the faults of others, but we forgive and forget. This has the power to cover sin and even to stop the destruction caused by taking offense and reacting. The one who sins is also impacted by our willingness, from our purified heart, to forgive and treat the person as though he or she had not offended us.

4. What further insight is found in the verses below?

Proverbs 10:12

Proverbs 17:9

While Peter is being theological, Proverbs offers straightforward, practical wisdom. When we just "let it go" and forgive offenses, we avoid further trouble, sin, and strife.

5. In what ways do you think love can cover sin? Can you think of a

situation where you have witnessed this?

6. Reread John 3:16 and Romans 5:8. What is it that sets God's love

apart—that makes it so extraordinary?

"Earnest" love (1 Peter 1:22) is what sets this apart. It is one thing to try to ignore offenses, but another to seek out someone for the purpose of showing love. God loved so much that He could not ignore our plight as sinners.

Even now, He seeks us out to demonstrate His love to us. This earnest, passionate love changes us. We are to emulate this and see the impact it has on the ones we love.

DAY 3: CARE AND KINDNESS

1. When you think about those who join you in worship and fellowship at your church, do you think of them as family? Why or why not?

2. Read Romans 12:10 and James 4:11 and then answer the questions below:

   What relationship is emphasized?

   How are the "brothers" to be treated?

❖ James tells us how powerful our tongue is. We can use it for great evil or for good. We must surrender control of our tongue to the Lord so it doesn't cause us to damage others.

We are "family" in Christ; and we love each other as brothers and sisters. For some of us, this is no comfort because our own families are painful places. We may have even learned to act out of "love" in a very dysfunctional way. The Romans 12:10 passage mentions "brotherly affection." God is working to transform you and me into people who deeply care for our fellow Christians and act in their best interests.

3. The Body of Christ (the Church) has no small or unimportant

members. As part of His body, we treat every member the same,

giving the same love, care, and honor to everyone. How does

1 Corinthians 12:25 support this truth? (Read verses 12-27 for a full

context.)

4. What does Ephesians 4:2-3, 32 teach you about how to relate to

other believers?

The fruit of the Spirit produces a unique set of relationship skills. The gentle way we relate with each other and the humility that takes the spotlight off us is remarkable. We become incredibly patient with one another—overlooking offenses and "putting-up" with each other in a loving way. This is one of the ways "love covers a multitude of sins" (1 Peter 4:8). We choose not to focus on the wrongs, hurts, faults, and things that might otherwise cause us to have relationship problems.

5. Write out 1 Thessalonians 3:12.

Over time our love should be growing for our brothers and sisters. This Thessalonians passage points to the source of the love that grows in our heart—the Lord working in us, causing our love to abound.

Thinking about the kind of love you've studied so far may be very humbling. Always remember, our Lord kindly says to us, "we love because He first loved us" (1 John 4:19). You cannot just conjure up this kind of love on your own. Where you fall short, go to Him. He is the Source of this love!

6. Write a prayer to God, praising Him for the redemption He provides, confessing your relational sins, and asking for Him to create in you a heart of love.

DAY 4: SERVE

1. Based on what you have studied thus far, why is "loving one another" so vital in the Church?

2. Why is loving each other difficult?

3. How can you truly love your Christian family? (Be specific in your answer.)

4. Read the verses below, and then note what you learn about "loving one another."

1 John 3:11

1 John 3:23

1 John 4:7

1 John 4:11

1 John 4:12

Consider this:
  • The most basic one-another idea is that we must love each other:
    * It is a commandment from our Lord.
    * God is the source of our love. He is love. (See 1 John 4:8, 19.)
    * It is evidence to the world that we are Christ's followers (John 13:35).
    * Since He so loved us, we are compelled to love others. (See John 3:16 and 1 John 4:11.)

- While the word *love* is used ubiquitously in English, and has almost lost its meaning, this word is powerful. In the Greek, the word in all the listed 1 John passages is *agape*—a love that "can be known only from the actions it prompts" (*Vines Expository Dictionary of Old and New Testament Words*, Fleming H. Revell Co., Old Tappan, New Jersey, vol 3, pg 21). God showed us this love powerfully in giving His Son to be the substitution for our sins. (See 1 John 4:9-10.)
- We demonstrate our love (*agape*) when we act on behalf of another, for the good of another.
- God wants to reveal Himself to others through us. He empowers us with His love to impact the world for their good and His glory.

5a. Knowing what Christ has done for us and equipped us to be, how do we respond, according to:

Romans 13:8

Galatians 5:13-14

b. How are we not to respond, according to 2 Corinthians 10:12?

> ❖ "Anyone who does not love does not know God, because God is love. In this the love of God was made manifest among us, that God sent his only Son into the world, so that we might live through him. In this is love, not that we have loved God but that he loved us and sent his Son to be the propitiation for our sins. Beloved, if God so loved us, we also ought to love one another . . . . We love because he first loved us" (1 John 4:8-11, 19).

> ❖ "For God so loved the world, that he gave his only Son, that whosoever believes in him should not perish but have eternal life" (John 3:16).

6. In Luke 10:25-37, our Lord is asked how one might "inherit eternal life." The "correct answer" is love God with all you have and are; and your neighbor as yourself. Jesus used one of the greatest stories of all time to answer the question, "Who is my neighbor?"

   While the story of the Good Samaritan is not about one Christian loving another, it is a perfect demonstration of the kind of love we are to have for each other. He cared. He acted. Verse 37 may be the most important one in this passage: "you go, and do likewise." What is it the Lord wants you to "go and do"?

DAY 5: WHAT ABOUT YOU?

Whether it is our home as a child or an adult, a longtime work situation, or our church, relationships—in close proximity—are the proving ground for who we really are.

Because the situations are unpredictable and out of our control, over time, these real-life situations may bring our "real selves" to the surface:

- Revealing who we really are and moving us beyond platitudes and pretense;

- Testing the depth of our character by pushing us to our relational limits; and

- Exposing our true emotions in the stress of crisis or conflict.

However, these situations not only serve as a proving ground in the sense that they reveal, but they also can strengthen:

- Helping us learn and grow through both successes and failures; and

- Refining our strengths as we develop skills through real-life application.

As we deal with other people in life, we make choices that shape us. If we allow ourselves to be overtaken by anger and frustration, we will almost certainly develop deep resentment and bitterness. Resentful, bitter people tend to wound those around them, and their attitude becomes a gift that keeps on giving. If, because of our fear, we learn to avoid responding at all, we may hide emotionally for the rest of our lives.

The world is filled with people who are hurting and who struggle in every relationship. They have seldom seen healthy interaction or conflict resolution. They are the walking wounded.

Use the following questions to prepare—mentally, emotionally, and spiritually—for your growth in Christ. Be prayerful and honest as you answer. If this study is going to be transformational, it must begin with an assessment of the areas where we really need to change. For some, this may be difficult.

1. On the scale below, how would you rate your life situation as you grew up?

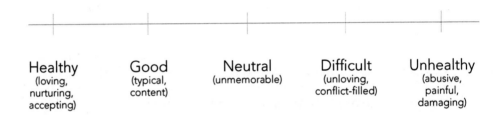

Healthy
(loving,
nurturing,
accepting)

Good
(typical,
content)

Neutral
(unmemorable)

Difficult
(unloving,
conflict-filled)

Unhealthy
(abusive,
painful,
damaging)

It is important to realize that living in this sinful world has impacted all of us. Even if our home life was picture-perfect, or seemed so, we will have areas of sin and struggle. No matter how mundane or dramatic our story, God has a plan to speak into our lives and transform us.

2a. The events, habits, etc. that occurred in our formative relationships will inevitably impact us in most all aspects of life. Although it may be uncomfortable or painful, honestly list some of the negative attitudes and relationship habits from your growing-up years that you carry with you now:

b. Can you see in yourself attitudes and sinful relationship habits you saw modeled as you grew up? (List and explain.)

c. In brief, how have these attitudes and habits affected your relationships at home, work, church, and other situations?

d. When you honestly think about how you "treat" others, especially those you love, what displeases God?

3. What relationship situations have recently tested you?

4. What are these tests revealing about who you really are? How does this compare to who you really want to be?

Relationship Situation	What It's Revealing	Whom I Want to Be

5a. List any steps you have taken to deal with negative or damaging attitudes or habits, which are detrimental to your relationship with God and others?

b. What needs to change for you to become the person you know you should be—the person you want to be?

❖ Devote time in prayer, asking God to help you be honest about your relationship challenges—impacting who you are and how you interact. As a result of this prayer and thought process:
- What sinful behaviors or attitudes do you need to confess to God?
- What relationships in your life need mending?
- Whom can you ask to help provide advice, counsel, and/or accountability?

❖ Write down an action plan to began dealing with some of these issues, if you haven't already begun to do so. Pray the Lord will help you through this study. Take at least one concrete step this week to begin dealing with an area where you know you need significant change.

WEEK TWO
FORGIVE ONE ANOTHER

"BE KIND TO ONE ANOTHER, TENDERHEARTED, FORGIVING ONE ANOTHER, AS GOD IN CHRIST FORGAVE YOU" (EPHESIANS 4:32).

Remember Jack—a Christian calloused by life's disappointments and the hurts received from others? The world is full of people just like Jack, and unfortunately, so is the Church!

No doubt, Jack is a hurt person. Actually, everyone is a hurt person. But Jack is also blessed, and we are all blessed people. So how does Jack—and you—reconcile the struggle between the hurt and the grace . . . to actually forgive?

DAY 1: FORGIVENESS

When you are hurt or angry at someone because he or she has offended or wounded you, you are in danger of becoming bitter. The bitterness, once it takes root, begins to corrupt your heart affecting your attitude and interactions with others. Releasing hurt and negativity through forgiveness brings the greatest freedom; but choosing to forgive may be the hardest choice you or someone you know, will ever make. As the adage goes, everyone is a fan of forgiveness until you must practice it.

Building on the principles discussed in Week One—our love for one another—the next one-another issue to consider is forgiveness.

Fundamentally, our forgiveness is based on the forgiveness God has provided for us:

- His pattern gives us an example we can follow.

- His power gives us the ability to forgive.

- His command gives us instructions to obey.

1. Read the passages below, note how God's forgiveness toward you impacts your forgiveness of others.

Matthew 6:12, 14-15

Ephesians 4:32

John 20:23

God is a forgiver. Jesus' example of giving us forgiveness is the critical foundation for our own forgiving heart and mind. Like Christ, we forgive the offenses of others. We rest in His forgiveness; and because we are forgiven, we forgive.

2. Read John 13:36-38; 18:15-18, 25-27; 21:1-19. What does this story teach you about forgiveness?

Jesus' forgiveness of Peter serves as a great example of how Christ's complete, unconditional forgiveness impacts a life. Our Lord did not just teach forgiveness, He modeled it. In the story you just read, Peter failed Jesus at one of the most crucial points in Jesus' life. He was under attack and alone. Even after Peter promised never to forsake Him, here His close friend denied and abandoned Jesus. This is an offense not easy to forget, much less forgive.

3a. How has God's forgiveness impacted your life?

b. Why does God's forgiveness in your life equip you to forgive others, especially fellow Christians?

4. In this lesson, we are sort of putting ourselves in Jesus' place—seeing Him as our model of how to forgive. But have you put yourself in Peter's place—the guilty one in need of forgiveness? Not only do we need to ask God for forgiveness, but we must also ask forgiveness from those we have offended and hurt. Whom do you need to ask forgiveness from? How will you, in obedience to Christ, ask for forgiveness?

WEEK TWO

DAY 2: UNLIMITED FORGIVENESS

1. What are the differences between God's forgiveness and people's forgiveness?

A poignant difference between God's forgiveness and our own is that His forgiveness is unconditional, while we often forgive on conditional terms:

- I'll forgive you if you grovel for it.
- I'll forgive you if you say you're sorry, and do this and that.
- I'll forgive you if justice is met.

We like the sound of forgiveness. We want others to forgive. We believe in forgiveness. But the pain of our hurt makes it difficult to overcome the offenses. And sometimes our standards of what is right or good make it difficult for us to forgive those who fail to meet them. The hurt, coupled with our sense of justice, often makes it seemingly impossible to forgive.

But what does the Bible teach about unlimited forgiveness? Is it only for God?

Read Matthew 18:21-35.

2a. What does this passage teach you about the *quantity* of

forgiveness?

b. What does this passage teach you about the *quality* of

forgiveness?

Jesus taught the disciples, and in turn us, that forgiveness has no limit when it comes from a pure heart. He wants us to learn to forgive sincerely and completely. In correlation with the teachings of Matthew 18, Colossians 3:13 says, "forgive whatever grievances you may have against one another" (NIV). Paul challenges us here to forgive whatever it is that we have against another—literally any complaint, quarrel, or grievance. There is no limit; nor any ifs, ands, or buts about it.

This is really challenging! If we take Colossians 3:13 literally, we are setting an amazingly high standard. People can do really awful, unimaginable things to each other. Does the work of Christ really provide the resources to forgive *anything* anyone does to or against us?

The challenge is for us to fall into His grace so deeply that He removes the results of the bad things people do to us. It is possible for God to change and heal us, even if the offender never changes or never asks for forgiveness.

Most of us will face situations where, in ourselves, we cannot muster the strength, or even understand how it is possible, to forgive. Here is where this becomes an entirely spiritual matter. It is humanly possible (amazingly so) for people to forgive offenses, but some things can only be forgiven as God gives the grace to do so.

3. God's power is the resource for forgiveness. He enables us to forgive when we cannot do so on our own. For insight on this truth, read these verses:

- Colossians 3:12-13. Paul is talking here about the transforming power of the gospel. It has the power to change our lives and make us completely different.

- 2 Corinthians 5:17. In the same way the power of the resurrection saves us, it then makes us compassionate, kind, humble, gentle, and patient. Add to the list—forgiving! The same power that raised Jesus from the dead is the resource for forgiveness. Of course you cannot save yourself, so also you cannot become like Jesus in your own power. Thus, stop trying to muster up forgiveness for those things you cannot forgive on your own; submit yourself and allow God to develop it in you.

And one more important note—forgiving is not the same as saying "what the person did is okay." In order to release the anger, bitterness, and emotional poison of something from your past, you may need to extend forgiveness for very sinful and destructive acts. You may pray something like this: "God, what that person did (to me or to others) was wrong, but I will leave You to judge and ultimately bring a reckoning. You have given me such overwhelming forgiveness that I trust You to help me forgive what this person has done and move on in Your grace."

4. Write a prayer to God, confessing: your hurts, pre-conceived ideas about forgiveness, reluctance to forgive others, etc. Ask Him to open your heart and mind to forgive those who have offended and hurt you.

WEEK TWO

DAY 3: PRACTICING FORGIVENESS

1. When it comes to extending forgiveness, what are your anxieties or concerns?

Putting forgiveness into practice may be harder than it sounds or seems. In many cases—especially for previous, older offenses—really embracing forgiveness may be a process. But how can you shed the apprehension and walk towards forgiveness?

2. Write out Ephesians 4:32.

❖ Will you take the challenge to memorize Ephesians 4:32?

Practicing the love discussed in Week One is the best way to learn to forgive practically. And, it can start with one who is easy to love. Jesus said more than once, "If you love me, you will keep my commandments" (John 14:15, 21; 15:10; 1 John 2:3-5; 5:3 just to name a few). He has commanded us to forgive; so if we love Him, we will want to be forgivers just as He is.

"Practicing" sometimes means what it implies: We get better at it by doing it. The "act" of forgiving usually precedes the feeling of genuine forgiveness. As with other areas for growth, God is faithful to honor our obedience in this process. You will be pleasantly surprised as God turns your desire to learn to forgive into genuine heart-felt forgiveness.

3. What are some situations where you need to apply this principle of "practicing" forgiveness (even if you can't fully embrace the feeling of forgiving)?

As we love Him and others, that love produces kind and gentle interaction flowing from a tender heart. This is what it means to be Christlike. Begin by:

- Building habits of kindness and tenderheartedness;
- Dwelling on the fact you've been forgiven; and
- Practicing forgiveness.

4. First Peter 5:7 reads, "casting all your anxieties on him, because
he cares for you." How do the truths learned in this verse
encourage you in your efforts to forgive others?

When we bring our concerns, hurts, and hang-ups to God and leave them with Him, God helps us to be able to forgive others. He cares for your hurts. And He cares for your soul. God doesn't want you to be poisoned by the venom of bitterness, hatred, or hurt.

5. How are you going to take step towards or extend forgiveness
this week?

DAY 4: REAL, PRACTICAL FORGIVENESS

1. Read the verses below, noting what they teach regarding how Christians are NOT to treat each other.

Matthew 7:1–5

Romans 14:13

1 Corinthians 6:7

As we love and prefer one another (Romans 12:10), we are willing to be wronged rather than bring a fellow Christian to justice. Although these verses may not be one-another passages in an instructional sense, they are an example of how we are not to treat each other; therefore, making them instructive.

2. Read Ephesians 4:2, noting what it teaches you about practical forgiveness.

"Bearing with one another" requires the ability to forgive each other. The NIV translation of Colossians 3:13 (from Day 2) renders the phrase, "forgive whatever grievances you may have against one another." Humble, gentle, and forgiving, meaning we do not allow others to irritate us. Literally, God's grace empowers us to "bear with" or put up with each other. We do not respond in anger or frustration. By God's grace and with His help, we forgive! This sets us apart as a Christian community.

When we interact with each other in life, there are often "empty spaces" between us, meaning there are gaps in understanding and information. People say and do things and we are not sure why. It is our natural tendency, often, to fill those empty spaces with suspicion or with negative assumptions. When we hear someone said or did something we don't understand, we might think: She did that because she wanted to hurt me. Or he said that to damage my reputation. Many relationships have been irreparably damaged because of such assumptions. Hurts have been taken on when the intent may not have been to hurt at all—perhaps often there is just a misunderstanding.

When grace is operating in our lives, we deliberately choose to fill those empty spaces with good assumptions. When Paul says "bearing with one another in love," he surely refers to the kind of love described in the classic passage, 1 Corinthians 13.

3. Read 1 Corinthians 13:4-7. Which of these descriptive phrases about Christian love help us fill the empty spaces with good things?

4. What situations in your relationships have empty spaces where negativity is developing (in you or perhaps you can see it in someone else)? What do you need to do to apply forgiveness?

As the Lord builds real forgiveness in our heart and minds, we grow to resist the strong, natural desire to change another person before accepting and loving them. It involves literally putting up with the shortcomings of the other person.

In marriage, family, and close working relationships, this is particularly critical because we can see the glaring faults of the other person. When we are truly forgiving, we learn to overlook faults and say: I will love and forgive, even if this person never changes.

This is the way God deals with our faults. He wants us to be Christ-like, and He works to change us. Nonetheless, He will still forgive us 70 times 7!

When we grow in Christ-likeness, we begin to adopt an amazing balance. We love and forgive, yet long to see those we love grow in grace.

The teaching of unconditional forgiveness is balanced by other biblical truths. Think about this example:

> The Christian shop owner, learning an employee has stolen money confronts and dismisses the dishonest employee. Feeling remorse, the offender asks for forgiveness and promises, in repentance, to repay all she has taken. The godly owner immediately assures the former employee that all is forgiven, hopefully restoring the relationship. (The owner may even choose to forgive repayment of the loss in her graciousness.) Feeling the joy of restoration, the forgiven one asks for her job to be restored. But, her former boss refuses kindly. In the ensuing confusion, the godly owner instructs the forgiven one that she must now prove herself as being true to her word over time. Even though she has been forgiven, she has lost the privilege of trust for a time.

Sometimes we will have to honor biblical truths that lead us to make decisions not to extend trust to those who have done wrong. This may be true in church, business, friendship, and even family relationships. As grace allows us to fill the empty spaces with good things, the truth (that closes the information and understanding gaps) may compel us to use good and godly judgment, which might result in correction or even necessary separation. Forgiving and putting up with each other is, in this way, balanced by other godly principles.

DAY 5: THE BENEFITS

1. What are some of the physical, spiritual, and emotional side effects of unforgiveness you have observed? Which of these have you experienced in your own life?

2. What are some of the physical, spiritual, and emotional benefits of forgiveness you have observed? Which of these have you experienced in your own life?

The side effects of unforgiveness may be anger, bitterness, hatred, spiritual regression, physical illness, stress, sleepless nights, and on and on. Yet, the benefits of forgiveness are peace, joy, contentment, spiritual growth, freedom, etc. So, why not forgive!

3. Read Proverbs 14:10; Ephesians 4:20-32; and Hebrews 12:14-15.

Why do these verses urge believers to forgive others?

Face it, an unforgiving heart and mind stunts your spiritual growth, even impacting your emotional and physical health. God does not want this for you. He wants to help you grow in His grace by extending forgiveness to others. Roll up your sleeves, cast your care upon God, and do it—forgive.

WEEK THREE

SUBMIT TO ONE ANOTHER

"Submitting to one another out of reverence for Christ" (Ephesians 5:21).

Fundamentally, Jack is inferior. At least, that's how he feels. Because of past hurts he feels unloved and unworthy. To compensate for this, he has adopted a tough-guy approach in dealing with authority and with anyone who is asking him to submit in any way.

Jack bucks at people who want him to conform or do what they say. It's not rebellion; it's pride. Others see and describe him as "just really stubborn." Deep inside Jack feels like he does not measure up. So, he is regularly compensating for this by being "his own man," independent and unyielding.

He has been overcome by pride. It's the plan the enemy has used to make his life less effective than it could have been. For Jack, it is actually his insecurity—something no one would be "proud" of—that has been the stimulus for his pride.

DAY 1: CLOTHED WITH HUMILITY

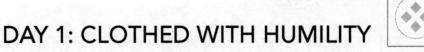

Humility is central to the one-another verses; it is absolutely imperative for this week's study—submitting to one another! While you can pull off some of the other one-another commands without humility, you cannot submit without it. Of course, you might submit to people because you feel inferior to them or you are afraid of them, but genuine, biblical submission requires a work of grace in our lives.

For all sorts of reasons, the idea of submission has gotten a bad reputation. For some people, the concept of submission suggests the idea of a master and a slave or of an overbearing parent or a domineering spouse who ruled the home sternly.

But what does God's Word say about submission?

1a. Write out 1 Peter 5:5.

b. What does this verse teach you about your interaction with other Christians?

Grace makes interpersonal relationships work within the Body of Christ, while our pride is the enemy of the right kind of godly relationships. As we humble ourselves—that is, we become honest about our own weaknesses and sinfulness—God's grace begins to flow. It is not natural, and maybe not at all possible for us to "put on" humility by ourselves. It is by God's grace this can happen.

2. In your opinion, how does submission to God result in submission within the Church?

When we choose to submit to the Lord, something amazing happens—self begins to fade from prominence. Any person, who sees himself and his needs as primary, cannot walk in a submissive way. Submission is deferring; it is putting yourself and your needs as secondary to those of others or to a higher cause.

3. According to 1 Peter 5:2-3, how are church leaders to serve in action and attitude?

Submission is not just for followers. Leaders must serve as humble examples to those they serve.

In this 1 Peter 5 section, Peter is giving practical instructions to church leaders, encouraging them to serve with the right kind of attitude. To these primary leaders, he tells them to lead with humility and not to be domineering.

4a. In verse 5, Peter turns to the younger ones, perhaps future

leaders. What is his counsel for them?

b. Why is this an important principle?

> ❖ You cannot be an effective Christian leader until you have learned to follow others humbly with the right attitude.

In verse 5, Peter goes on to speak to everyone (young and old alike): "Clothe yourselves, all of you, with humility toward one another." Peter is helping us understand, through practical instruction that the Christian community functions well when it is powered by humility. Not just humility from those who are younger with less experience, or those who have lesser positions.

The Bible is full of examples that help us see the value of a humble spirit. We also know from life experience that humble people are easier to deal with and to get along with. But this passage takes it into the realm of spiritual reality. Almost stated as a law, certainly as a truism—Peter tells us something about God that we really need to know if we are to navigate life successfully. It's almost like Peter is saying: "Don't you realize? God opposes the proud but gives grace to the humble."

5. Write out Proverbs 8:13. Is this verse startling to you, why or why not?

God hates pride, and He actively works against it! God is actually working against pride and pride-driven people. By contrast, He is on the side of the humble. Humility will always be accompanied by His active support. When a church is full of humility, the free-flow of God's grace is unrestrained.

6. Spend time in prayer, asking God to point out areas of pride in you. Ask Him to create a humble spirit in your life.

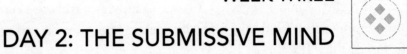

DAY 2: THE SUBMISSIVE MIND

1. Read Philippians 2:5-11. Philippians 2 provides us with an understanding of our Lord's motivation—Why did Jesus do it? Why did He become one of us? Paul does not write Philippians 2 just so we can know it, but so that we can emulate it. In this passage, Jesus is presented as our model.

2. What do you glean from Paul's statement in Philippians 2:5?

If you want to be Christ-like, you need to understand how He thinks. You need to adopt His way of thinking. Do you think like Christ?

Further, when Paul says we need to share our Lord's thinking, he is being specific. We need to imitate how Christ thought about Himself. Philippians 2 is about how Jesus saw Himself, and as an extension, how we need to see ourselves.

3a. Read verse 6. Knowing Jesus is God, what does this verse teach you about His sense of entitlement and what He valued?

b. What does verse 7 say about His attitude toward Himself?

c. What does verse 8 teach about how His way of thinking influenced His actions?

d. How do verse 9-11 support the passages on humility (1 Peter 5:2-5 and Proverbs 8:13) studied in Day 1?

Looking at this passage, we can see that the kind of submission described in the New Testament is a Christian grace. It is part of the work of sanctification—where God makes us more like Jesus. In fact:

- We submit because that's what He models for us.
- We submit because it glorifies God when we do.
- We submit, because through our submission, God creates beautiful relationships and breaks down those things that divide us.

4a. How do the realities of Philippians 2:6-11 impact you?

b. In what areas do you need to take on the mind of Christ?

c. Continue praying about cultivating this essential attribute in your life.

DAY 3: REVERENT SUBMISSION

1. Based on what you have studied so far, what is the point or the purpose of submission within the Church?

It is important for us to see submission as intentional. It does have a purpose. God values humility and submission. He does not just want to have a church that is active and growing where people are being saved and taught. He does not just want work and "success." God wants His people to be obviously different. When His people demonstrate the kind of humility that puts others first—undeniably putting themselves last—they are doing something "other-worldly." This is what Jesus was like, and it was extraordinary. It is a godly attribute that shows we are His and we are powered by something people of this world do not have.

2. It's easy to understand what submission means when we think about a king and his subjects or even a parent-child situation. But, what do you think it looks like for Christians to live in submission to one another?

So far, we've learned:

- Submission is a grace.
- Submission requires humility.
- Christ is our model for the submissive mind and life.

3. What does Ephesians 5:21 teach you about submission? What motivates godly submission?

Ephesians 5:21 is preceded by: "giving thanks always and for everything to God the Father in the name of our Lord Jesus Christ." As we minister to each other and live as thankful people, we submit to each other in our interactions and body life. This mutual submission forms the basis for the relationships Paul then describes in the following verses (marital, family, etc.).

We submit to each other because we *revere* (KJV renders the word *fear*) Christ. As a person practices godly submission to others, he or she honors Christ in the way he or she lives and interacts with others.

"Submit" is literally to yield or subordinate ourselves. We choose a lower place as Christ, our model, did. Remember Philippians 2:7-8: "Made himself nothing, taking the form of a servant . . . he humbled himself by becoming obedient to the point of death, even death on a cross."

4. Are you choosing to subordinate yourself to other believers in so doing giving honor and reverence to the Lord Jesus Christ? Why or why not?

DAY 4: THE SUBMISSIVE, INTERDEPENDENT COMMUNITY

Our culture promotes independence and perfection, causing many to hide weaknesses, insecurities, and sin in attempts to go-it-alone flawlessly. Yet, we need each other . . . not just sometimes, but every day. Living in the kind of community to which God has called us requires us to walk in humble submission to each other.

1. Read Romans 12:3-21, listing all the ways we are to behave in our community of believers.

2. How does James 5:16 support the idea of Christian community? Why is it important to be this vulnerable and humble with other believers?

3. In contrast, what does Galatians 5:26 teach you NOT to do?

The KJV renders the Galatians passage as "let us not be desirous of vain glory." Empty conceit or desire for self-glorification leads to terrible treatment of each other. We annoy, irritate, and provoke each other, wanting what another has (possessions, talents, relationships, etc.). All of this is because we are not focused on glorifying Christ or on the other person.

It is important to note that God is the one who distributes our talents and spiritual gifts. Then, we place people in positions based on God's giftedness. They are to accept those positions with humility, recognizing God is the one who gave the gift. Others submit to them—out of reverence for Christ—understanding what is good for the body is good for individuals. In so doing, each submits to God's will by submitting to others in the positions God has placed them.

4. How have the truths studied today challenged you in any

relationships you have within your church?

DAY 5: PRACTICAL SUBMISSION

How does one who has been given major responsibility and authority—a senior pastor, CEO, the president, etc.—demonstrate a submissive heart and mind? Follow this logic:

1a. What does Galatians 3:27-29 teach about our place in Christ? What is the significance of those characteristics we focus on so much (race, religion, status, etc.)?

b. What does Romans 12:3-4 teach us about how we received our gifts and abilities? Is it a result of something we have done?

c. How should these ideas shape the way leaders in the church view themselves?

If anything, the understanding that we are all the same in Christ and He is the One who has chosen to give us the gifts and positions we have, ought to make leaders more humble. The deference and submission given to leaders is because of God, not because they are more worthy than those who follow them.

2. So, how does a leader demonstrate the proper spirit?

3. How can you demonstrate a submissive heart and mind to fellow brothers and sisters in your church?

4a. Read John 13:1-17. How is Christ's humility demonstrated here? What does this passage teach you about submission?

b. How can you—even this week—"wash someone's feet"?

WEEK FOUR

PRAY FOR ONE ANOTHER

"PRAY FOR ONE ANOTHER" (JAMES 5:16).

When he hears the prayer list read in church, Jack's heart winces. He knows many around him are struggling with sickness, sadness, and much more. He bows his head and closes his eyes, but he doesn't have much to say to God. People ask for prayer, and Jack says: I'm praying for you. But he doesn't mean it.

God knows his mistakes, his sin. Why would God want to hear his prayers? What can Jack say to God to help anyone's situation?

His nonchalance and guilt about prayer makes him wonder—does anyone really pray? Does prayer make a difference? He pushes his mind to other places as he thinks: Does anyone pray for me?

DAY 1: PRAYER IS FOUNDATIONAL

Can you really change? You may have given up hope for anything better—anything more authentic—in your relationships with other believers. This week's study is meant to tackle this issue by focusing on one of the greatest tools in the universe for genuine change—prayer. Even if you are walking closely with the Lord and He has freed you from the things Jack struggles with, prayer is for you. Some of the most amazing characteristics and behaviors in the one-another passages can only be realized through prayer.

And, prayer not only changes us, but it is our only hope of seeing some things change in others. In case you haven't realized it, you cannot change other people. No amount of manipulation, begging, pouting, or wishing can change another person's heart—only God can do this. There will be some relationships and people in our lives as Christians that we will simply have to commit to God through prayer.

The same is true with circumstances. Our lives will be greatly impacted by things totally out of our control. We will be left to respond and sometimes, to just pick up the pieces. God has given us prayer so that we can survive, even thrive, no matter what we face in life.

Very few people are the expert "pray-ers" they wish to be. Most have never experienced all God wants for us in this spiritual activity.

1. When you think about prayer, what comes to your mind (not

   necessarily a definition)? Write down your thoughts.

For many, guilt is at the top of the list. If we are honest, some of us pray rarely or only when we want something or are in trouble. You might honestly say you are confused about prayer or it makes you a little uncomfortable. Maybe you pray, but you know you are not experiencing all the joys and benefits of a full prayer life. Does your prayer life need some work?

One-another passages are about God making us into the image of His Son. In this area of prayer, as well as those previously studied, our Lord is the example—not just as a person who prayed, but also as one whose entire life was built on prayer. Prayer was central and foundational to Jesus. No one can really understand the life and ministry of Jesus without seeing His commitment to prayer. Jesus lived as though His life depended on prayer.

2. Read the following passages and answer the corresponding

   questions:

a. Mark 1:32-37. Describe how Jesus deals with the exhausting

   demand of His new public ministry. What is the significance of

   prayer in relationship to ministry?

b. Luke 6:12-13. How long does Jesus pray on this occasion? What can you learn from this event about the importance of prayer for Jesus personally and in relation to ministry and important decisions?

c. Luke 11:1. How was Jesus a model for His disciples to emulate? What can we learn from this?

d. Luke 22:39-46. At the most intense moment of His life, Jesus turns to the Father in prayer. His agony is obvious. Ultimately, what is His prayer, and what can you learn from it?

Prayer was not an activity, good work, or obligation for Jesus. It was His lifeline. He wanted to be in the presence of His Father through prayer. For Jesus, prayer was critical in at least two important ways:

- It was how He stayed relationally connected to His Father.

- It was His source of power for His ministry.

3. Describe your prayer life in light of Jesus' example.

4. If Jesus, the Son of God, needed this prayer connection with the Father, how much more do we? Maybe there is a commitment you need to make regarding your own prayer life. Write out the reasons you need to change your prayer habits. Compose a prayer of commitment asking for God's help.

DAY 2: BECOMING A PERSON OF PRAYER

Jesus, our Lord and model, introduced the world to a different kind of spirituality. His teachings confront most of our ideas about "religion" and literally turn them inside-out. Religions are sometimes fixed on external things like rites, rituals, and symbols. In Jesus' day, the leaders of their faith were super-religious. Yet Jesus was not impressed. Over and over, He went to the "heart of the matter."

1. Read Matthew 5:8; 15:8. In chapter 15, we're jumping into a situation where Jesus is correcting the religious leaders of His time. What exasperated Him about their "religion"? What kind of faith does He want?

Jesus makes it clear in this passage and in all His teachings that He is most concerned about our inside—our heart. A genuine follower of Christ is one whose heart is fully engaged in His faith. He does not just "do" or say religious and Christian things. To please Him, it is necessary for us to "be" genuine in our motivations and heart attitude. He wants us to be real, not just to seem Christian.

In no other area of our faith is this more relevant than in prayer. Saying, "I will pray for you," is easy. Real prayer on behalf of the needs of others is harder. Since, for the most part, prayer is private and personal—no one sees or really knows how real our prayer life is.

Read Philippians 4:6-7.

2a. What critical life lesson does Paul's instruction give us for how to

handle our worries, crises, and struggles in life?

b. Describe the person who lives life consistent with this passage.

Does this describe you?

c. What benefits are explicit and implicit in this teaching for the

person who decides to deal prayerfully with life's circumstances,

decisions, and challenges?

d. How do you need to apply what you've learned from this

passage? What current circumstances and situations will you deal with according to the wisdom you've gleaned here?

God has given us the gift of prayer. He invites us to bring everything to Him—whatever troubles or frightens us. He promises to care, to guide, and to listen.

God is calling all of us to care and make a difference in prayer. Although it may seem selfish, before we can do that for others, we need to look at our own need for prayer. Until we align ourselves with God, we will be ineffective in praying for others.

Hebrews 13:15 tell us to continually offer the sacrifice of praise to God. What does this mean? We can learn from some examples:

❖ In prayer, we must:
• Practice praise.
• Practice confession.
• Practice thanksgiving.

3a. Read Psalm 8:1-9; 34:3. How can you magnify the Lord in prayer?

b. Read Daniel 9:4-19. How did Daniel praise and magnify the Lord

   in prayer?

Because He is worthy to receive it and we, as His people, need to give it. Praise is adoration of God and giving Him the honor He deserves. We do not need to teach or remind God of how great and awesome He is, but we need to be reminded. Praise "puts us in our place" as it honors God as the Creator, Sustainer, and Lord of our lives. We submit ourselves to Him and His rule over us.

4a. Because living in this world corrupts us, we need to be

   "cleansed." Read Psalm 24:3-5. What are the requirements

   listed for coming into the presence of God?

❖ "Clean hands" is clearly a reference to our actions and behaviors. "Pure heart" refers to our motives.

b. Read 1 John 1:9. How do we meet the requirement of Psalm 24:3-5?

5. Read Ephesians 5:17-20. What do you learn about your prayer life from these verses?

This passage is one of those where we are explicitly told what the "will of God" is for all believers. Verse 20 makes it clear that it is God's will for us to constantly give thanks to Him for everything in the name of Christ. We can and should give thanksgiving to Him because He is the provider of everything in our lives (James 1:17).

The passage we studied earlier, Philippians 4:6-7, instructs us that as we are praying about everything in our lives, we are to do so with an attitude of thanksgiving (verse 6). The genuine follower of Christ has a prayer habit that is permeated with thanksgiving.

6. How can you apply praise, confession, and thanksgiving to your prayer life?

WEEK FOUR

DAY 3: INTERCESSION

In addition to praise, confession, and thanksgiving, another component in prayer is supplication. The simplest idea of this word is "humbly asking for something." When we ask in this way for others, we call this intercession.

1. What does it mean to intercede?

2. Read John 17. For whom is Jesus interceding? Based on this

   chapter, summarize some ideas of what it means to pray in an

   intercessory way.

3. Read Romans 8:34 and Hebrews 7:25. What do these verses help you understand about Jesus' current ministry?

> ❖ Being Christlike means being an intercessor. Even now, His ministry is interceding to the Father for the needs of His followers.

4. What hinders you from being an intercessor for others?

5. When thinking about interceding for other believers in prayer, avoid using that as a cover or excuse to gossip about, judge, or belittle another. Read Galatians 5:15, another one-another passage. What are we NOT to do?

When we are selfish, we can become critical. Our one-another interaction becomes focused on each other's shortcomings and flaws—even in prayer! As we target these, we can attack each other with criticism and other negative interactions that destroy us. Our interactions with and prayers for fellow Christians should be ones of love, truth, and good will.

6. Write out some things you need to change in your intercessory prayer life:

DAY 4: BEARING ONE ANOTHER'S BURDENS

Of all the concepts unique to Christianity, the idea of community is perhaps one of the most impacting. Caring about each other is the foundation of Christian fellowship (which we study in Week Five). God uses our care for each other as the glue that holds a Christian community together. Praying for the needs and concerns of another person is an act of this type of caring.

1a. Write out Galatians 6:2.

b. What does the instruction found in this verse mean?

2a. How does prayer fulfill this directive to help "bear" the burden of

another?

b. What sorts of burdens do people have that we need to help them

bear through our prayers?

The law of Christ is the law of love. Like Him, we put the other person first. In this, we serve the need of the other. Bearing the burden of another is actually caring about someone else enough to become involved in his or her life.

One of the most effective ways for us to "bear the burden" of another is through prayer. We share in the burden-bearing ministry of the Holy Spirit (Romans 8:26-27) and the intercessory ministry of Jesus (Romans 8:34).

3. The context of Galatians 6:2 is restoring a person who has fallen

into sin. Based on this context, what kind of "burden" are we

asked to help bear for a brother or sister?

4. The language in Galatians 6:1 uses the imagery of prey ensnared in a trap. How can we help bear the burden of someone "ensnared" in sinful actions or habits through our prayers?

5. Read Luke 22:31-32. What can you learn about praying for victory over sin from the Lord's example?

Fighting against the temptation to sin is warfare. In the case of Peter, the Lord says Satan is lurking, waiting to destroy Peter. Later Peter would write, "Be sober-minded; be watchful. Your adversary the devil prowls around like a roaring lion, seeking someone to devour" (1 Peter 5:8). Peter knew he had an enemy.

You (and those you care for) are at war. We pray for strength against temptation, whether it comes from the world (1 John 2:15-17), our own flesh and passions (James 1:14), or the devil.

6. We love with God's love so much so that we come alongside the sinning person and we help that person carry "his" or "her" burden—making the other person's problem ours! How is this contrary to our natural reaction to a Christian in sin?

7a. Summarize James 5:14-15.

b. What can you learn about dealing with sickness in the community
   of faith?

c. What are some of the ways we minister to the sick person?

Many prayer times in churches involve praying for physical needs of
people. We are obviously impacted by the immediate needs in our lives,
and it's natural for us to be fixed on them. God understands this. Jesus
was concerned about the sickness and disease around Him. He ministered
to these needs while caring for the entire person. His followers should do
the same.

DAY 5: TRANSFORMING INDIVIDUALS AND COMMUNITIES

Because of the complexity of people, we cannot change another person. Yet prayer is a powerful weapon for changing people because it brings God into the equation. Paul says in 2 Corinthians 10:4-5 that our spiritual "weapons," including prayer, are "mighty," and they can literally break strongholds. Bitterness, addictions, gossip, rage, hatred, broken relationships—these are all strongholds that destroy our brothers and sisters and eventually our community. We often feel powerless against their destructive forces. But we have the promise that prayer changes things.

Paul is such a great example of a minister who prayed for his brothers and sisters. Whatever was happening in their lives and in the churches he loved, he took it to the Lord in prayer and trusted God would be working in the spiritual realm as he was doing all he could in his daily ministry. We need more people in our churches praying earnestly for one another and fewer people who are spending their time pointing out the things that need to change.

1a. Read Philippians 1:9-11. What does Paul pray for the Philippian

Christians?

b. How might a prayer like this benefit the people you know?

2. Read Ephesians 1:15-23, listing what Paul prayed for.

Paul's greatest prayer for his brothers and sisters in Christ was spiritual wisdom and power for ministry. He prayed the gospel over their lives and saturated his desires for them with truth.

3. Studying the topic of prayer is beneficial. Contemplating application of prayer is beneficial. But all is in vain, if we don't pray. Will you take this challenge? Select a member in your study group to put on your "prayer list," and begin implementing what you have learned about prayer. Commit to pray for this person for the remainder of the study (and even beyond!). Write a prayer for him or her below.

WEEK FIVE

FELLOWSHIP WITH ONE ANOTHER

"But if we walk in the light, as he is in the light, we have fellowship with one another, and the blood of Jesus his Son cleanses us from all sin" (1 John 1:7).

Although he's attended his church for 17 years, Jack often still feels alone. While he is at church, he does feel connected to those he's known for so long, but that feeling soon fades as everyone exits the sanctuary, marching back into everyday life and busy schedules. The jokes and "how are yous" leave off at the door just to be rehashed next Sunday.

Jack hasn't experienced the family-like relationship that exists in the Body of Christ, primarily because he's never learned to love, forgive, submit to, or pray for fellow Christians in his church community; so, how could he ever really fellowship with them?

DAY 1: REDEMPTION—
THE POWER FOR COMMUNITY

"Fellowship" is one of those *Christianese* words rarely heard outside the church. Although fellowship is a churchy concept, we in the Church have often failed to really live it out as God intended. In some churches, fellowship only means a social activity involving casseroles and surface-level conversation.

It's a shame because fellowship is a really beautiful concept. It comes from the Greek word *koinonia*, which means literally "sharing in common" (*Vines Expository Dictionary of Old and New Testament Words*, Fleming H. Revell Co., Old Tappan, New Jersey, vol 2, pg 90). It is the idea of a life-sharing that emerges within a group of Christians because of what they have in common—because of the ways they are the "same." The social interaction (and the casseroles) should be the symptoms or the outworking of something much deeper.

These days people can better understand the concept of "community." When properly understood, community is a great euphemism for the New Testament idea of fellowship. We "do life together" as an interdependent, sharing, and loving community.

The Apostle Paul painted a beautiful word picture to help us understand the concept of sharing in common. We are a body, Paul says (1 Corinthians 12). We are not independent, but interdependent. We need and rely on each other. Without each other, we are incomplete and cannot accomplish God's plan for His Church. Each of us is significant and vital to the whole. If you are simply a member of a church and not a part of this kind of community, you are not experiencing what God designed for you.

1. As you begin this lesson, assess your current situation honestly. Circle the description that best fits your experience right now (thinking about involvement in a Christian community of fellowship):

Isolated	Attending	Involved	Connected
I believe I am a Christian, but I feel alone in my faith.	I go to church, but I am not connected with people other than when I attend.	I have some connection, but relationships are on the surface; I need to go deeper.	I am blessed to be in a real community with deep friendships. We are living life together.

Ever wonder why people group together? When you think about people who share something in common and on this basis they group together, what is the root of their connection?

2. Think of some groups and what draws them together. Using the example given, list a few more you are aware of:

Group	What they have "in common"
MADD (Mothers Against Drunk Driving)	People involved are committed "To stop drunk driving, support the victims of this violent crime and prevent underage drinking." (http://www.madd.org/About-Us.aspx)

Isn't it interesting to think about what pulls people together? You may have thought of groups that come together only for a season of life or a limited time. You may have thought of some that involve people for a lifetime. Some have strong connections, but are limited to only one or two areas of their lives, while others to connect people at every level.

What about the church?

The fellowship described in the New Testament is amazing, deep, and life changing. What is the basis for this fellowship?

3a. Read 1 John 1:3, 5-7. According to verse 3, what is John's purpose in writing this letter?

b. As he explains his "message" in these verses, what is John presenting as the basis of our mutual fellowship?

As you can see from this passage, the idea of biblical fellowship is much more than surface-level friendship. John is inviting us into a deep connection—one he shares with God. The basis of our connection is "light." John says, "This is the message we have heard from him and proclaim to you, that God is light, and in him is no darkness at all." He compels us to "walk in the light, as he is in the light," and says if we do, we will share this fellowship. What we have in common is light, which is God's righteousness.

We can share fellowship with God and each other because we have been made righteous by the blood of Christ. Consider these passages:

- Ephesians 2:13—But now in Christ Jesus you who once were far off have been brought near by the blood of Christ.

- Romans 3:23-24—For all have sinned and fall short of the glory of God, and are justified by his grace as a gift, through the redemption that is in Christ Jesus.

- 2 Corinthians 5:21—For our sake he made him to be sin who knew no sin, so that in him we might become the righteousness of God.

- Romans 5:9—Since, therefore, we have now been justified by his blood, much more shall we be saved by him from the wrath of God.

Each of these passages is rich if you look at the full context. But for the purposes of this study and our commitment to fellowship, it is enough for us to understand that Jesus Christ died in our place on the cross to make us right with God—justified. It is this justification that is the foundation for genuine Christian fellowship. When we say there is "power in the blood," or we talk about the "power of the resurrection," it is not just effective in saving us from our sins; it is a power that brings us into fellowship and community, overcoming anything that might divide us.

4. Describe what it means to you that you have something "in common" with other believers. What does that mean for the way you are choosing to live?

DAY 2: COMM-*UNITY*

1. Write out John 17:21. What is Jesus' prayer for His followers?

While diversity is less of a challenge for some groups, it can be a real complication for the church. Can you imagine a skeptic listening to Jesus' prayer for unity from John 17? If he or she understood what Jesus was asking, what might his or her reaction be? Is it even possible to achieve the unity Jesus is asking for, especially when it involves these dimensions and differences:

- People from different socio-economic backgrounds?
- People from different racial and ethnic backgrounds?
- People from different cultural traditions?
- People with differing political ideologies?

All of these diverse people developing the kind of unity that creates in them "one heart," and "one mind" seems like a dream, an impossible dream to some. Jesus' ideas on this subject are revolutionary. He is clearly talking about something beyond just a group or a club. His Church is a place where people are transformed in such a way that the *result* is "oneness." In the church, we are fellowshipping and doing life together on the basis of being strongly unified in spite of our clear surface differences.

When you think of God's plan to create unity, not only is our diversity as people a challenge, but there is also an even greater obstacle. If diversity were the only issue, then people who are "alike" should get along well. Has that been your experience? Is there always unity in your home? How about in the homes of others you know?

2a. Read Galatians 5:16-24. As Paul explains the work of the Holy Spirit in overcoming the "flesh" and giving gifts, he lists the "works of the flesh." List some of these works that make unity difficult.

b. Can you think of examples where these "works of the flesh" have been a hindrance to the unity God wants for us?

c. Which of the fruits of the Spirit listed in these verses help to create unity?

d. Summarize in your own words the challenge to unity among

Christians presented by the sinful nature.

> ❖ Remember 1 John 1:7? "But if we walk in the light, as he is in the light, we have fellowship with one another, and the blood of Jesus his Son cleanses us from all sin." The sinful nature is not an insurmountable obstacle to our fellowship and unity— Jesus Christ has provided a way for us!

3a. Read Psalm 133:1 and Philippians 2:1-2. What is it that

makes God (and Paul, like Christ in John 17) full of joy?

b. How is it possible for people to come together with

nothing else in common except Christ and live out the kind of

unity He is presenting here?

4. Write out a prayer of commitment stating what you plan to do,

as God works in you, to stimulate unity with other believers and

create the sense of community and fellowship God intends us to

share.

DAY 3: AGREEMENT AND HARMONY

As we study the various dimensions of the one-another passages, it becomes clear they are not all distinct and separate ideas. They are complimentary and interactive. As we look at these ideas, we realize the work of becoming Christ-like is less like a checklist and more like a full makeover. As He makes us like Him from the heart, good things flow out of us.

1. Write out these one-another verses:

Mark 9:50

Romans 12:16

Romans 15:5-6

2 Corinthians 13:11

2. What do you learn about "harmony" with other Christians from these passages?

Living a life that demonstrates Christ requires all of us to have unity so we can impact the world. We must live together in peace for our community to impact the world.

Through humility we live together in harmony. Peaceful relationships are the result of His working humility in us. We are not too proud to associate with anyone. We defy the natural "pecking order," where socio-economic factors drive our interaction and pride so easily enters in.

"Haughty" in Romans 12:16 can be high-minded, meaning proud of who we are, who we associate with, or what others might think of us. The enemy of our harmony and godly relationships is our pride. Paul warns us not to think too much of ourselves in Romans 12:3a—"For by the grace given to me I say to everyone among you not to think of himself more highly than he ought to think, but to think with sober judgment."

Humility gives us sobriety in our self-assessment. In fact, agreement is the basis of our peace and harmony with each other as we focus on putting Christ first in our lives. When we always seek our own way, we find it challenging to agree. But, when we seek the good of another, we work toward agreement. This requires the "it's-not-about-me" attitude.

Our peaceful relationship with our Lord reflects itself in our harmonious relationships with others as Christians. When we as believers live in harmony with each other, we reflect so well on the Father that He is glorified. It begs the question "who would not want to live in a loving, supportive, harmonious community?" People will want to know a God who produces this result.

The Scripture teaches, rather clearly, that part of our fellowship with one another involves the truth that God wants His people to live in harmony, even more—to live in agreement.

So, what is the secret? You may be asking yourself the question: "Okay, if we are all going to agree, then that means someone's opinion, idea, or proposal will win and then the rest of us will have to comply, or give-in—right?"

Is it really a win-lose situation? How can there possibly be a sense of genuine agreement that results in anything that could be described as "the same mind?"

Maybe we think: "Okay, then we must select the right leader who will bring us a vision from God so we can all know the direction we must take; and then we can all have the same mind—right?"

It's tough, isn't it? We like the idea of fellowship when it means being together as Christian friends. But, what about this idea that our harmony and agreement is so pleasing to God we become the answer to Jesus' prayer in John 17?

There is no formula for this kind of harmony. To be clear, there is no sure-fire, step-by-step model for handling every potential disagreement. Remember, the one-another teachings are about making us like Christ. When a disagreement begins to arise, imagine if everyone involved was more concerned about other people and glorifying Christ than having his or her own way. When a potential conflict arises, imagine someone wanting peace and harmony more than he or she wants to get his or her way.

The key to this harmony and having "one mind" is found in a familiar verse we studied in Week Three: "Clothe yourselves, all of you, with humility toward one another, for 'God opposes the proud but gives grace to the humble'" (1 Peter 5:5b). When we seek our own way, or look for vindication, we are on our own. But, when we humbly want to glorify the Lord and seek the good of another God is at work among us. His grace flows freely in our relationships and He develops harmony, oneness, and even agreement.

3. Think about how this looks in a church. Is this operating in your church? Is this operating in your life? What can you do to be a catalyst for this in your home and among your fellow believers?

4. Acts 2 records the day of Pentecost and the coming of the Holy Spirit to indwell believers. Read Acts 2:42-47, which follows that dramatic event and is basically a commentary on the Christian community at the time. Do you think this group could be described as having the "same mind?" How was this achieved?

5. Although these early believers may have taken communal living beyond what the Scriptures call for, what can you learn about the Holy Spirit's impact on creating unity, harmony, agreement and fellowship among Christians from this story?

6. What do you need to do as a result of this day's study to contribute to the harmony and agreement in your community of believers?

DAY 4: SHOW HOSPITALITY

Hospitality may be a dimension of fellowship that comes more naturally to us. It is not a leap to think about hosting people in our homes as an aspect of fellowship. This is true; however, Christian hospitality is much deeper than that.

1. Read Romans 15:7. How are you to welcome others? How has

   Christ welcomed you?

"Welcome" in Romans 15:7 literally means "to take to one's self" (*Vines Expository Dictionary of Old and New Testament Words*, Fleming H. Revell Co., Old Tappan, New Jersey, vol 3, pg 255). We might use the phrase "take in" to imply a similar meaning—welcoming someone into your home and family. God receives glory when we take each other into our friendships, homes, and lives. The warmth of this type of fellowship is a unique characteristic of passionate Christ-followers.

2a. Write out 1 Peter 4:9.

b. Why are we prone to grumble when showing hospitality?

c. Why do you think we shouldn't grumble, both with our mouths
and in our minds?

In this verse, "hospitality" means generosity, giving. One must possess
an unselfish heart to practice this virtue. Christians, because of their pure
hearts, should demonstrate this more than any other group of people.

We are prone to grumble because of our selfishness. We want for ourselves
and because of this are hesitant to share our resources/things or what we
value (like our time).

Peter charges us to realize we are different because of the work of Christ.
We are also living in a temporary situation here on earth as pilgrims; our
real home is the afterlife in heaven. So, we must adopt heavenly values and
reject those around us in our temporary home. One of these values is loving
our brothers and sisters and sharing what we have with them.

3. Do you view hospitality as a command or just a good idea for Christians? Explain your answer.

Hospitality is a command for Christians. It is expected. In a list of miscellaneous instructions, Paul includes this one: "Contribute to the needs of the saints and seek to show hospitality" (Romans 12:13). Even though hospitality is sometimes considered a spiritual gift, it (like evangelism) is the responsibility of every Christian. Those with the special gift will naturally excel and even lead the rest of us in this area, but we are all to be hospitable.

4. How is God working in your life to welcome others as He welcomes you?

5. What areas of selfishness do you need to ask God to help you overcome?

DAY 5: BREAKING GOD'S HEART

1a. Throughout the study, we have looked at various "negative" one-another passages—instructions for the ways we are not to treat one another. Read the following Scriptures. Beside each reference, write what it teaches you about how NOT to treat fellow Christians:

Romans 14:13

1 Corinthians 6:7

2 Corinthians 10:12

Galatians 5:15

Galatians 5:26

Colossians 3:9

James 4:11

James 5:9

b. What theme do you see running through these passages?

Having put on Christ-likeness, we do not operate in the "old ways" as Colossians tells us. Good deeds and good intentions are not the common denominator in such behavior—Christ is. It is through Christ and His work in us that we can put off the old behavior and put on the new. Thus, Paul exhorts his readers to treat each other like Christ would—to be truthful, encouraging, hospitable, and so forth with one another.

2. Read Romans 16:16; 1 Corinthians 16:20; 2 Corinthians 13:12.

Although these traditions may seem unusual to our 21ˢᵗ century

culture, why do you think Paul urged such actions?

For anyone who has traveled extensively around the world, these ideas will not be as odd. Common greeting practices in some places might be very uncomfortable, even a bit offensive to people from other regions. These passages written by Paul speak of a warm greeting used, especially when believers partook of the Lord's Supper, as a sign that their fellowship was unbroken by some of their disagreements. Paul deals with divisions and lack of unity throughout 1 Corinthians that needed to be overcome by the love of Christ.

3a. Read Ephesians 4:1-3. How do these verse challenge you?

b. How do they encourage you?

❖ Memorize Ephesians 4:1-3. The truths of this passage can encourage you as you grow in relationship within your church.

c. How can you apply these truths to your church relationships?

WEEK SIX

MINISTER TO ONE ANOTHER

"AS EACH HAS RECEIVED A GIFT, US IT TO SERVE ONE ANOTHER, AS GOOD STEWARDS OF GOD'S VARIED GRACE" (1 PETER 4:10).

Recently Jack actually listened to a sermon on rewards. His pastor taught about the joy Christians will have when they receive rewards for their good works—for acting Christ-like here on earth. He had never thought much about the subject (maybe that's why he stayed awake).

What brought a tear to his eye was the part where the pastor said Christians would take their rewards—their crowns—and place them at Jesus' feet as an act of worship. The concealed tears and the lump in his throat were there because, in spite of all his coldness and apathy, Jack knows what Jesus did for him. He is sure Jesus loves him, even if no one else does.

Jack thought, "I'd really like to do something to make Jesus smile." He wondered—what kind of ministry could someone like me do for Jesus?

DAY 1: MINISTRY = MEETING NEEDS

Like the word *fellowship*, "minister" is another word we use more at church than anywhere else.

1. What do you think it means to "minister" to one another?

Sometimes we associate the word *minister* with people who pursue church work as their vocation. In the New Testament the word *minister* or *ministry* is used more than 30 times (ESV). The same word often translated "minister" is also sometimes translated "servant." Thus, in its simplest definition, ministering is serving.

2. What does ministry NOT mean? Read Galatians 5:15, 26, and

then read Romans 14:13; Colossians 3:9; James 4:11; and James

5:9. How do the one-another behaviors in these passages work

contrary to ministering to one-another?

As we interact with one another, the "works of our flesh" are almost our natural (default) settings. Of course, we are selfish, and, of course, we attack when we feel frustrated or threatened. It's almost like there is a "survival of the fittest" instinct built into our sinful nature that works to advance our cause while combating others. Thus, it's not very natural to minister to each other.

3. Be honest, what are some of the things in your life—and perhaps

your personality and habits—that make it challenging for you to

minister?

In Galatians 5, where we looked at some negative one-anothers, we learn the secret to a life that demonstrates ministry characteristics: "But I say, walk by the Spirit, and you will not gratify the desires of the flesh" (Galatians 5:16). Rather than giving in to our flesh, we submit ourselves to God and allow His Spirit to direct us.

As in all of the attributes we are studying, Jesus is our model for ministry. We learn how to submit to the leading of the Holy Spirit, by seeing how He did it.

4. Read John 13:12-17. The story in John 13 is an amazing picture of Jesus Christ, the Servant Leader. What do His words in these verses teach us about Christ's service to His disciples, His attitude, and His ideas about putting ministry into practice?

We need to follow the example of our Lord and serve one another in humility. Jesus' decision to wash their feet provided a real service for them (one typically done by a servant). He also did this as a symbol of the way He wants us to give humble service and ministry to meet each other's needs.

Jesus' ministry was directed at the needs of people. Our Lord was keenly aware of people's needs, and then ministered to them. He not only saw the needs they expressed, but He cared about their deeper needs. He exemplified these teachings:

Mark 10:45	For even the Son of Man came not to be served but to serve, and to give his life as a ransom for many.
1 Corinthians 10:24	Let no one seek his own good, but the good of his neighbor.
Philippians 2:4	Let each of you look not only to his own interests, but also to the interests of others.

5a. Read Galatians 6:1-2. What ministry is described in these verses?

b. What is the "law of Christ?"

c. How do you think this law is fulfilled practically?

The law of Christ is the law of love. When asked about the greatest commandment in the law, Jesus said the entire law was summed up in loving God and loving others (Matthew 22:35-40). Like Jesus, we put the other person first, serving his or her need. The context of Galatians 6:2 is restoring a person who has fallen into sin. We love with His love so much that we come alongside and minister to the person who has failed and we help him or her carry "his" or "her" burden, making the other person's problem ours.

Remember in Week Four, we looked at this passage pointing out that prayer is an effective way to help bear the burdens of another. There is certainly more to it than prayer—in some cases, God allows us to provide accountability, encouragement, instruction, and many hours of time to help restore a person who has been "caught" in a sinful pattern.

6. Are you regularly putting the needs of others (starting with

fellow believers) ahead of your own? What do you need to do to

become a person who, like Christ, is passionate about ministering

to the needs of others?

DAY 2: USE YOUR GIFTS IN
SERVICE TO OTHERS

So, how does one get started in ministry? How do you know which needs you're supposed to meet and what ministry you're supposed to perform? Although you may be unsure, when you reach the place in your Christian experience that you're asking these questions, this is a great sign. It means you're getting it. Every Christian is supposed to be a minister!

1. Read Ephesians 2:8-10. This classic salvation passage not only tells

   us how one becomes a Christ-follower, but it also gives insight

   into our destiny. What does verse 10 teach us?

As His hands and feet, we are to make this world better (salt of the earth), increasing the "goodness quotient" in this world, turning evil into good. This is ministry—doing the "good works, which God prepared beforehand, that we should walk in them."

So, back to the questions: Which needs, and what ministry?

As we've studied previously, in Romans 12 and 1 Corinthians 12, Paul describes the church as the Body of Christ. Read these verses and think through the accompanying questions:

2a. Romans 12:4-6 and 1 Corinthians 12:18. What insight do these verses give as to how your place and ministry in the body have been designed?

b. 1 Corinthians 12:25-26. What insights about God's design of the body and how it should function do you glean from these verses?

Each of us, as members of each other, function as part of this body and do various functions as do human body parts. God has given us the abilities/gifts that we are to use in our roles in the body.

In 1 Peter 4:10, we are told: "As each has received a gift, use it to serve one another, as good stewards of God's varied grace." One of the most important uses of our gifts is to serve our fellow believers. By referring to it as a "stewardship," Peter implies that we will be held accountable for what we do with our gifts. They are not our gifts; they are on loan to us from Christ. He expects us to use them to encourage and strengthen each other and to bring Him glory.

And in the traditional sense of stewardship, we are also to give financially to our brother and sister in need. We should view our finances as gifts from God too. As God blesses us monetarily, we give to aid others as an extension of God's provision and care.

Peter points out that grace is the operational force making our relationships and interactions work. Love produces (works in concert with) grace. We love, forgive, forget offenses, don't get "hung-up," give to, and simply serve each other. This makes the body function well together and creates the sense of community that God desires.

3. Thinking about your personality, passions, natural talents, and interests, what do you see as the gifts God has given to you for ministry?

❖ You get the sense that David reflects God's heart when he says, "Behold, how good and pleasant it is when brothers dwell in unity!" (Psalm 133:1).

4. What needs and opportunities can you see in the body that you can meet through your gifts?

DAY 3: COMFORT AND ENCOURAGE

Sometimes life seems like one problem after another. It's not possible to avoid these difficulties or the wounds that accompany them. When we are under the pressure of our problems, we are vulnerable—to temptations, discouragement, and giving up. All of us need comfort. As we function in the body, comforting each other is vital to our spiritual and emotional health.

1a. Read 2 Corinthians 1:3-4. What two titles does Paul give to God

in verse 3?

b. Describe how God ministers to us in our difficulties.

The word translated *comfort* (in nearly every translation) in the original is a compound word. Comfort is made up of these two ideas to "call" and "alongside." When we comfort someone we literally walk with him or her through his or her situation—at his or her side.

Tragic moments can be the major turning points in people's lives. Their reactions can either lead to negativity and despair or a proper perspective, becoming stronger and wiser. Comfort, not just platitudes or empty words, can make the difference.

The promise given to us in Romans 8:28 is a great basis for comfort. When we "know," as the verse says, that God is working all of the events, trials, problems, and situations of life together to create good, we can trust Him even when we do not understand what we're going through. Comforting brothers and sisters actually ministers the comfort of verses like this one!

2. Read 2 Corinthians 13:11. In this simple verse, Paul admonishes us to the ministry of comfort, which is an important Christian grace. Describe a situation where you received comfort from another believer. Have you practiced this grace? When?

❖ "Two are better than one, because they have a good reward for their toil. For if they fall, one will lift up his fellow. But woe to him who is alone when he falls and has not another to lift him up! Again, if two lie together, they keep warm, but how can one keep warm alone? And though a man might prevail against one who is alone, two will withstand him—a threefold cord is not quickly broken" (Ecclesiastes 4:9-12).

3. Comfort is coming alongside a person when he or she is in need or trouble. Describe how this happens:

4. Read 1 Thessalonians 4:18; 5:11. We do not just minister comfort to others when they are in trouble. These verses describe another way we comfort each other. Describe this ministry of comfort.

We need to continually ask: "What is something encouraging I can do or say for my brother or sister today?" The admonition "encourage one another" is a command to us as believers. It is not a suggestion.

5. How can you show obedience to Christ and comfort and encourage?

DAY 4: EDIFY AND TEACH

"Go therefore and make disciples of all nations" (Matthew 28:19a). Jesus Christ's last command to His disciples is to reproduce disciples as we take the gospel to everyone on the planet. Like the one-another passages, the Great Commission is about multiplying the number of Christ-like people in the world. Making disciples involves "teaching them to observe all that I have commanded you" (Matthew 28:20a).

1a. Read Colossians 3:16. What is the qualification for teaching and admonishing?

b. What do you think the phrase "Let the word of Christ dwell in you richly" means from a practical standpoint?

c. Does this characterize your life?

We are charged to grow and mature in our faith and our walk. So much of the New Testament is dedicated to inducing spiritual growth and discipleship. We cannot please God and become like Christ until we allow His Word to dwell in us. If He is the "Word" (John 1:1) and we are to abide in Him (John 15:4), this must be our top priority. Is it?

The Word of Christ (Scripture) is to dwell in us in the sense that it influences and changes us. We are, in turn, responsible to spur our brothers and sisters to growth and maturity as well. What we have learned we share with others. Life wisdom, learned through obedient application of the Word, should be imparted to others—this is discipleship. It is what Jesus did and commanded us to do.

2. Give an honest assessment of your current level on these three

scales:

Spiritual growth	Regressing ☐	Stuck ☐	Maturing ☐
Indwelling Word (reading, studying, and meditating)	Rarely Ever ☐	Sometimes ☐	Regularly ☐
Admonishing and teaching others	Not Influencing Anyone ☐	Sometimes ☐	Regularly ☐

There is definitely a direct relationship between the indwelling Word, our spiritual growth, and the impact of our ministry in edification (building up) and teaching.

3a. Who has ministered to you by "teaching and admonishing you?"

b. Describe how you have done this for others.

Romans 15:14 says, "I myself am satisfied about you, my brothers, that you yourselves are full of goodness, filled with all knowledge and able to instruct one another." Part of our relationship with fellow believers includes sharing what we know with them so we all grow. Your spiritual maturity should be as important to me as my own: "Let each of you look not only to his own interests, but also to the interests of others" (Philippians 2:4).

4. Think through "sharing what you know." How does that take off the pressure to be a biblical scholar or ease your fears when thinking about implementing this one-another?

5. What do you need to do to begin living out this important one-another teaching?

DAY 5: WORSHIP WITH AND EXHORT ONE ANOTHER

Sometimes when unbelievers look at Christians, they see us as "religious." And sometimes "religious" is meant pejoratively (not a compliment). Many may think of us as weak or needy. They see religion as a "crutch," and they want nothing to do with it.

What onlookers see as "rituals," such as gathering together and singing songs or repeating prayers, we see as spiritually valuable and life-giving.

1. In Ephesians 5, Paul is teaching about the concept of being "filled with the Spirit" (5:18). One of the results of this Spirit filling is in verse 19; what is it?

2. Spirit-filled Christians worship, that is clear. But, there's a one-another component to worship. As we worship together, we encourage each other. How do you think this happens?

If you are not attending and fully engaged in corporate worship, you need to be. If you're there, but you're really not there, ask God to help you see the power of corporate worship. As we "address one another in psalms, hymns, and spiritual songs," we convey comforting and encouraging truths. We are drawn together, giving each other strength.

3. Not only do we gather together to worship, but there is also another reason we gather together. Read Hebrews 10:24-25. In verse 24, what are we instructed to do for each other?

❖ We worship God together because He is worthy of our adoration.

❖ We worship God together because it strengthens us personally.

❖ We worship God together as an encouragement to each other.

In this passage, the KJV uses the word *provoke* to describe this one-another ministry. It can mean, "irritate." The ESV reads "stir up one another to love and good works." However it is translated, it is an active attitude of provocation. As we gather with each other (the idea in this passage), we are to be catalysts for each other—helping our brothers and sisters to step out and take risks, be intentional, and serve the needs of others. The passage challenges us to make a habit of getting together to encourage each other to act for the sake of the gospel!

4a. Is this kind of exhortation happening in the gatherings at your church? What are you doing to encourage and provoke (in an edifying way) your brothers and sisters?

b. What do you need to be doing?

5. We are not only told to exhort each other to good works, what does Hebrews 3:12-13 encourage us to do for each other?

Overcoming temptation and sin is our daily struggle. "Exhort" here means to come alongside a person to strengthen him or her. We are each other's encouragers and cheerleaders in the challenge of dealing with sin. The encouragement of a brother or sister can help keep the heart sensitive to sin and help avoid the hardness that habitual sin brings. A true friend seeks us when we are in sin and exhorts us to be obedient to Christ.

6a. Are you connected closely enough with other believers to exhort them to overcome temptation?

b. Do you have brothers or sisters helping you to be victorious?

c. What is your plan/pattern of regular accountability?

As we come to the end of our studies, it is critical that we make sure we have strong relational connections with other Christians. Our ministry to one another must be the natural outflow of our strong, loving relationships. If we are to love, forgive, submit to, pray for, fellowship with, and minister to each other, we must be in close relationship and connection.

7a. What are you doing every week to make sure you are in strong relationships with your brothers and sisters?

b. What steps do you need to take today to strengthen your one another connections?

In the introduction to the study, it was said that churches tend to be places of conflict, dysfunction, and pain. We reassure ourselves by saying things like "Christians aren't perfect, just forgiven." While that is certainly true and comforting, it can be a cop out. If the needy and hurting people around us are going see Christ in us, it will not be because we are as messed up as they are, but (unlike them) we have a ticket to heaven. It will be because in some small, but extraordinary ways, we are like Him. Our Lord means to change us in the here and now so He can impact this needy world through us.

And it is of great comfort to remember too that we cannot obtain this Christ-likeness on our own—no good deeds, followed rules, or services attended will secure holiness. That is only found in the work of Christ and through the Holy Spirit working in us to produce fruit. The key to Christian "success" is through humility and dependence.

We can see so much of His plan to change us in these one another passages we've studied together. Hopefully, having completed this study, you have:

- Looked honestly at how much your life and character reflect the qualities and attributes of Christ.

- Identified things that need to change—ways you need to be transformed into the likeness of Jesus.

- Begun to allow Him to make some of those genuine changes in you.

Please do not stop!

Our prayer is that the six weeks of this study have opened your heart and mind to some new realities. People all around us need to see that the gospel is true and real. God means for them to see it through you and me. Imagine if your life and mine reflected the love of Jesus so clearly that it attracted people to trust Him and be set free!

By this all people will know that you are my disciples, if you have love for one another (John 13:35).

NOTE TO
LEADERS

Visit **www.randallhouse.com** and receive a **free Leader's Guide** for *Grace in the Empty Spaces*. Discover tools to aid you in leading your church or small study group through a six-week journey that is centered on the instructions in Scripture on how to treat one another.

To order additional copies of *Grace in the Empty Spaces* call **1-800-877-7030** or log onto **www.randallhouse.com**.

Quantity discount for 24 or more copies at $8.99 each.

FIRST AID FOR YOUR EMOTIONAL HURTS BOOKLETS

Addiction; Depression; Finding Help; Grief
by Dr. Edward J. Moody
Booklet

$4.99 each

Addiction
ISBN 13: 9780892656295

Depression
ISBN 13: 9780892656301

Finding Help
ISBN 13: 9780892656318

Grief
ISBN 13: 9780892656325

Excellent resource to reach those who are hurting.

Dr. Moody, author of *First Aid for Emotional Hurts,* is following up his successful book to pastors and laypeople seeking to reach out to help people with a series of booklets addressing specific issues people face. The booklets contain a biblical model for recovery and give appropriate resources for problems requiring professional help. The author also provides contact information for many sources providing help. Dr. Moody speaks with a qualified voice to the emotional, physical, and spiritual needs in various situations faced in today's society.

Dr. Edward J. Moody is on staff as an educator at North Carolina Central University, serving as an Associate Professor since 1995 and has chaired the Department since 2001. He also serves as the pastor of Tippetts Chapel Free Will Baptist Church in Clayton, NC. He is a National Certified Counselor, Licensed Professional Counselor in NC, Licensed Health Services Provider—Psychological Associate in NC and a Licensed Psychological Examiner in TN. Dr. Moody has published several articles in scholastic journals and serves as a workshop leader and conference speaker for various events within the religious community as well as the medical community.

To Order: (800) 877-7030
randallhouse.com

CPSIA information can be obtained at www.ICGtesting.com
Printed in the USA
241182LV00003B/26/P